Dear Mum

Written by

Teresa Heapy

Illustrated by

Agnese Baruzzi

OXFORD

UNIVERSITY PRESS

OXFORD
UNIVERSITY PRESS

Great Clarendon Street, Oxford, OX2 6DP, United Kingdom

Oxford University Press is a department of the University
of Oxford. It furthers the University's objective of excellence
in research, scholarship, and education by publishing
worldwide. Oxford is a registered trade mark of Oxford
University Press in the UK and in certain other countries

British Library Cataloguing in Publication Data
Data available

ISBN: 978-0-19-835635-6

10 9 8 7 6 5 4 3 2 1

Paper used in the production of this book is a natural, recyclable product
made from wood grown in sustainable forests. The manufacturing process
conforms to the environmental regulations of the country of origin.

Printed in China by Hing Yip

Acknowledgements

Series Advisor: Nikki Gamble

The publisher would like to thank the following for permission to reproduce photographs:
Cover: Ksanawo/Shutterstock; My Life Graphic/Shutterstock; **p1**: Ksanawo/Shutterstock;
My Life Graphic/Shutterstock; **p2-3, 4-5**: RTimages/Shutterstock; rprongjai/Shutterstock;
xtl974/Shutterstock; **p6-7**: Gary Yim/Shutterstock; **p7**: jointstar/Shutterstock; **p8-9**: Gary
Yim/Shutterstock; Ekaterina Pokrovsky/Shutterstock; Eric Isselee/Shutterstock; My Life
Graphic/Shutterstock; **p10-11, 12-13**: Alexander Vershinin/Shutterstock; Sergio Ponomarev/
Shutterstock; Milosz_G/Shutterstock; My Life Graphic/Shutterstock; **p14-15, 16-17**: Ksanawo/
Shutterstock; Madlen/Shutterstock; Willem Havenaar/Shutterstock; **p18-19**: Christopher Elwell/
Shutterstock; Eric Isselee/Shutterstock; Sipandra/Shutterstock; **p21**: Eric Issele/Shutterstock; My
Life Graphic/Shutterstock; **p23**: My Life Graphic/Shutterstock; **p24**: RTimages/Shutterstock; Eric
Isselee/Shutterstock; Madlen/Shutterstock; Willem Havenaar; rprongjai/Shutterstock

Dear Mum,

We've gone to the rainforest. But
don't worry, we'll be back by bedtime!

We're on a quest to find four gems.
Lord Zonktron has hidden the gems.
We have to get them back!

Love,

Anna and Joe

3

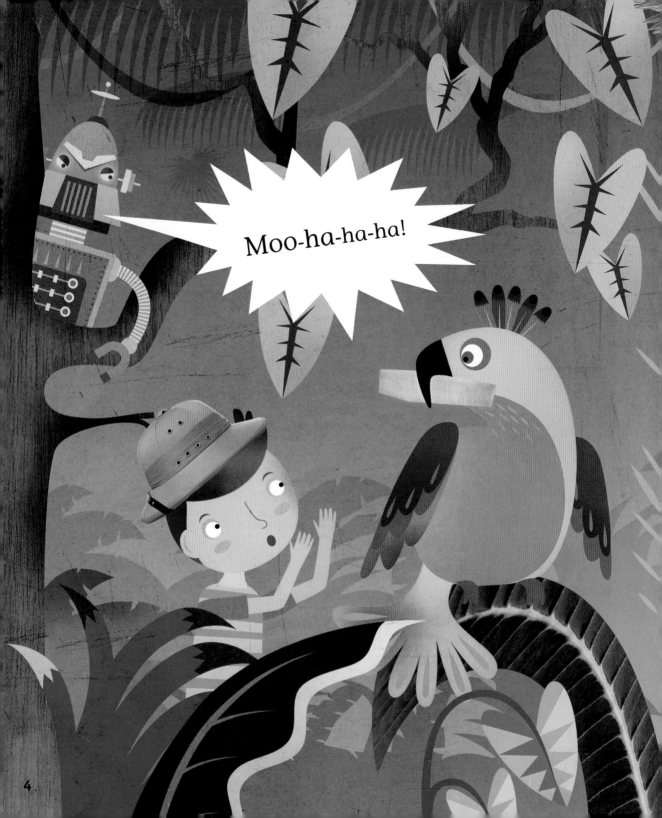

Dear Mum,

Lord Zonktron hid the gems in different places. He left us some clues to help find them.

We looked in the rainforest first. A parrot gave Joe the first clue!

This quest will turn you hot, then cold.

We're somewhere hot now. That means the first gem must be hidden somewhere cold!

Love,
Anna and Joe

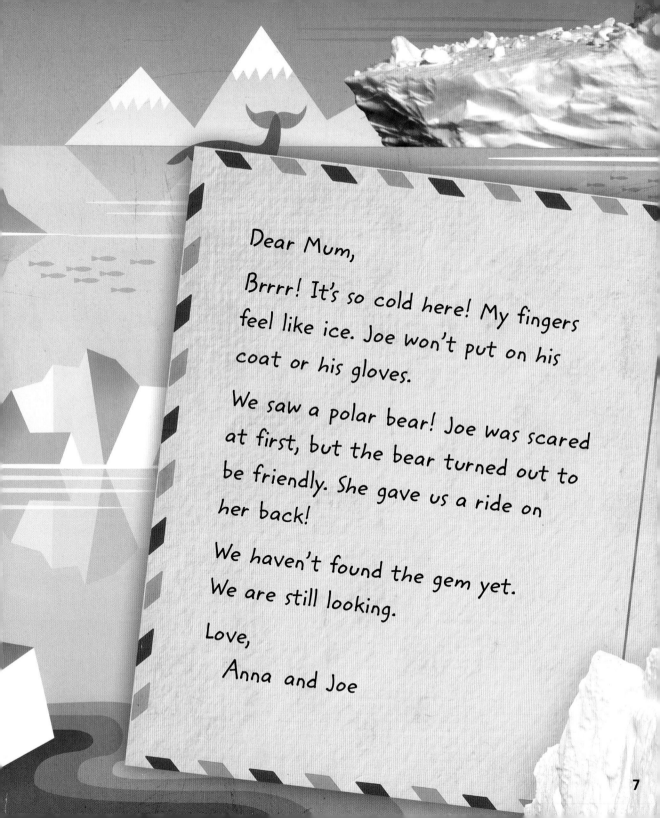

Dear Mum,

Brrrr! It's so cold here! My fingers feel like ice. Joe won't put on his coat or his gloves.

We saw a polar bear! Joe was scared at first, but the bear turned out to be friendly. She gave us a ride on her back!

We haven't found the gem yet. We are still looking.

Love,

Anna and Joe

Dear Mum,

We're still here in the snow!

I spotted a puffin. The puffin had the gem.

We did a dance for the puffin and he gave us the gem. He gave us the next clue, too.

To get to the next gem you will need a spade.

I think we need to get off the ice and start digging!

Love,
Anna and Joe

Dear Mum,

It's so dark! I'm writing this by torchlight because we're underground!

We heard something **rustling** in the darkness. Joe went to find out what was making the noise. I hope he's OK.

Love,
Anna and Joe

rustle

rustle

Dear Mum,

It was a mouse making the rustling noise.

A massive mouse!

Joe gave her a piece of cheese and I patted her. The gem was tied to her collar. She had the next clue, too!

The next gem is out of this world.

I think we'd better start digging our way out.

Love,
Anna and Joe

Dear Mum,

Wow! Now we're in space!
There's a really colourful planet near
us. We think the gem is there.

Joe is just landing on the planet.
I'd better go and join him!

Love,
    Anna and Joe

Dear Mum,

We're on the planet and we've made another friend. She's an alien! We played football with her.

Joe scored the winning goal. The alien gave him the gem as a prize. Then we found a clue stuck to the ball!

The last gem is in a creepy castle.

Oh no, I think that's Lord Zonktron's castle!

Love,

Anna and Joe

Dear Mum,

This really is the creepiest castle ever!

We can see the last gem. It's in the middle of a big maze. But Lord Zonktron's in there, too!

I hope we don't get lost! I think we might need some help...

Love,
Anna and Joe

18

Dear Mum,

We did it!

All our friends came to help. We found our way through the maze and got the gem.

We've got all four gems back now.

Hooray!

Love,
   Anna and Joe

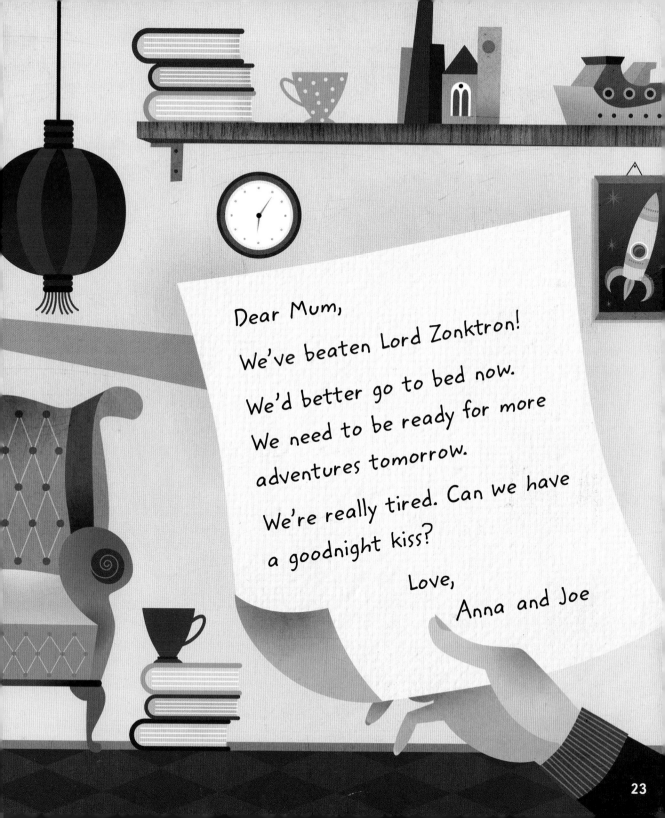

Dear Mum,

We've beaten Lord Zonktron!

We'd better go to bed now.
We need to be ready for more
adventures tomorrow.

We're really tired. Can we have
a goodnight kiss?

Love,
Anna and Joe